‘. . . a good bit of spice to give the critlings a flavour, and plenty of treacle to make the mince-meat look rich.’

HENRY MAYHEW

Born 1812, London

Died 1887, London

MAYHEW IN PENGUIN CLASSICS

London Labour and the London Poor

HENRY MAYHEW

Of Street Piemen

Edited by
Christopher Gangadin

PENGUIN BOOKS

PENGUIN CLASSICS

Published by the Penguin Group
Penguin Books Ltd, 80 Strand, London WC2R 0RL, England
Penguin Group (USA) Inc., 375 Hudson Street, New York, New York 10014, USA
Penguin Group (Canada), 90 Eglinton Avenue East, Suite 700, Toronto, Ontario, Canada M4P 2Y3 (a division of Pearson Penguin Canada Inc.)
Penguin Ireland, 25 St Stephen's Green, Dublin 2, Ireland (a division of Penguin Books Ltd)
Penguin Group (Australia), 707 Collins Street, Melbourne, Victoria 3008, Australia (a division of Pearson Australia Group Pty Ltd)
Penguin Books India Pvt Ltd, 11 Community Centre, Panchsheel Park, New Delhi – 110 017, India
Penguin Group (NZ), 67 Apollo Drive, Rosedale, Auckland 0632, New Zealand (a division of Pearson New Zealand Ltd)
Penguin Books (South Africa) (Pty) Ltd, Block D, Rosebank Office Park, 181 Jan Smuts Avenue, Parktown North, Gauteng 2193, South Africa

Penguin Books Ltd, Registered Offices: 80 Strand, London WC2R 0RL, England

www.penguin.com

This selection published in Penguin Classics 2015
001

Set in 9/12.4 pt Baskerville 10 Pro
Typeset by Jouve (UK), Milton Keynes
Printed in Great Britain by Clays Ltd, St Ives plc

A CIP catalogue record for this book is available from the British Library

ISBN: 978-0-141-98024-9

www.greenpenguin.co.uk

Penguin Books is committed to a sustainable future for our business, our readers and our planet. This book is made from Forest Stewardship Council™ certified paper.

Contents

Of Street Piemen

The itinerant trade in pies is one of the most ancient of the street callings of London. The meat pies are made of beef or mutton; the fish pies of eels; the fruit of apples, currants, gooseberries, plums, damsons, cherries, raspberries, or rhubarb, according to the season – and occasionally of mince-meat. A few years ago the street pie-trade was very profitable, but it has been almost destroyed by the 'pie-shops,' and further, the few remaining street-dealers say 'the people now haven't the pennies to spare.' Summer fairs and races are the best places for the piemen. In London the best times are during any grand sight or holiday-making, such as a review in Hyde-park, the Lord Mayor's show, the opening of Parliament, Greenwich fair, &c. Nearly all the men of this class, whom I saw, were fond of speculating as to whether the Great Exposition would be 'any good' to them, or not.

The London piemen, who may number about forty in winter, and twice that number in summer, are seldom stationary. They go along with their pie-cans on their arms, crying, 'Pies all 'ot! Eel, beef, or mutton pies! Penny pies, all 'ot – all 'ot!' [. . .] The pies are kept hot by means of a charcoal fire beneath, and there is a partition in the body of the can to separate the hot and the cold pies. The 'can' has two tin drawers, one at the bottom, where the hot pies are kept, and above these are the cold pies. As fast as the hot dainties are sold, their place is supplied by the cold from the upper drawer.

A teetotal pieman in Billingsgate has a pony and 'shay cart.' His business is the most extensive in London. It is believed that he sells 20*s.* worth or 240 pies a day, but his brother tradesmen sell no such amount. 'I was out last night,' said one man to me, 'from four in the afternoon till half-past twelve. I went from Somers-town to the Horse Guards, and looked in at all the public-houses on my way, and I didn't take above 1*s.* 6*d.* I have been out sometimes from the beginning of the evening till long past midnight, and haven't taken more than 4*d.*, and out of that I have to pay 1*d.* for charcoal.'

The pie-dealers usually make the pies themselves. The meat is bought in 'pieces,' of the same part as the sausage-makers purchase – the 'stickings' – at about 3*d.* the pound. 'People, when I go into houses,' said one man, 'often begin crying, "Mee-yow," or "Bow-wow-wow!" at me; but there's nothing of that kind now. Meat, you see, is so cheap.' About five-dozen pies are generally made at a time. These require a quarter of flour at 5*d.* or 6*d.*; 2 lbs. of suet at 6*d.*; 1½ lb. meat at 3*d.*, amounting in all to about 2*s.* To this must be added 3*d.* for baking; 1*d.* for the cost of keeping hot, and 2*d.* for pepper, salt and eggs with which to season and wash them over. Hence the cost of the five dozen would be about 2*s.* 6*d.*, and the profit of the same. The usual quantity of meat in each pie is about half an ounce. There are not more than 20 *hot*-piemen now in London. There are some who carry pies about on a tray slung before them; these are mostly boys, and, including them, the number amounts to about sixty all the year round, as I have stated.

The penny pie-shops, the street men say, have done their trade a great deal of harm. These shops have now got mostly all the custom, as they make the pies much larger for the money than those sold in the streets. The pies in Tottenham-court-road are very highly seasoned. 'I bought one there the other day, and it nearly took the skin off my mouth; it was full of pepper,' said a street-pieman, with considerable bitterness, to me. The reason why so large a quantity of pepper is put in is, because persons can't tell the flavour of the meat with it. Piemen generally are not very particular about the flavour of the meat they buy, as they can season it up into anything. In the summer, a street-pieman thinks he is doing a good business if the takes 5*s*. a day, and in the winter if he gets half that. On a Saturday night, however, he generally takes 5*s*. in the winter, and about 8*s*. in the summer. At Greenwich fair he will take about 14*s*. At a review in Hyde-park, if it is a good one, he will sell about 10*s*. worth. The generality of the customers are the boys of London. The women seldom, if ever, buy pies in the streets. At the public-houses a few pies are sold, and the pieman makes a practice of 'looking in' at all the taverns on his way. Here his customers are found principally in the tap-room. 'Here's all 'ot!' the pieman cries as he walks in; 'toss or Buy! Up and win 'em!' This is the only way that the pies can be got rid of. 'If it wasn't for tossing we shouldn't sell on.'

To 'toss the pieman' is a favourite pastime with costermongers' boys and all that class; some of whom aspire to the repute of being gourmands, and are critical on the quality of the comestible. If the pieman win the toss, he receives 1*d*. without giving a pie; if he lose, he hands it over for nothing. The pieman himself never 'tosses,' but always calls head or tail to his customer. At the week's end it comes to the same thing, they say, whether they toss or not, or rather whether they win or lose the toss: 'I've taken as much as 2*s*. 6*d*. at tossing, which I shouldn't have had if I had'nt done so. Very few people buy without tossing, and the boys in particular. Gentlemen "out on the spree" at the late public-houses will frequently toss when they don't want the pies, and when they win they will amuse themselves by throwing the pies at one another, or at me. Sometimes I have taken as much as half-a-crown, and the people of whom I had the money has never eaten a pie. The boys has the greatest love of gambling, and they seldom, if ever, buys without tossing.' One of the reasons why the street boys delight in tossing, is, that they can often obtain a pie by such means when they have only a halfpenny wherewith to gamble. If the lad wins he gets a penny pie for his halfpenny.

For street mince-meat pies the pieman usually makes 5lb. of mince-meat at a time, and for this he will put in 2 doz. of apples, 1lb. of sugar, 1lb. of currants, 2lb. of 'critlings' (critlings being the refuse left after boiling down the lard), a good bit of spice to give the critlings a flavour, and plenty of treacle to make the mince-meat look rich.

The 'gravy' that used to be given with the meat-pies was poured out of an oil-can, and consisted of a little salt and water browned. A hole was made with the little finger in the top of the meat pie, and the 'gravy' poured in until the crust rose. With this gravy a person in the line assured me that he has known pies four days old to go off very freely, and be pronounced excellent. The street-piemen are mostly bakers, who are unable to obtain employment at their trade. 'I myself,' said one, 'was a bread and biscuit baker. I have been at the pie business now about two years and a half, and I can't get a living at it. Last week my earnings were not more than 7*s.* all the week through, and I was out till three in the morning to get that.' The piemen seldom begin business till six o'clock, and some remain out all night. The best time for the sale of pies is generally from ten at night to one in the morning.

Calculating that there are only fifty street piemen plying their trade in London, the year through, and that their average earnings are 8*s.* a week, we find a street expenditure exceeding 3,000l., and a street consumption of pies amounting to three quarters of a million yearly.

To start in the penny-pie business of the streets requires 1*l.* for a 'can', 2*s.* 6*d.* for a 'turn-halfpenny' board to gamble with, 12*s.* for a gross of tin pie-dishes, 8*d.* for an apron, and about 6*s.* 6*d.* for stock money – allowing 1*s.* for flour, 1*s.* 3*d.* for meat, 2*d.* for apples, 4*d.* for eels, 2*s.* for pork flare or fat, 2*d.* for sugar, ½*d.* for cloves, 1*d.* for pepper and salt, 1*d.* for an egg to wash the pies over with, 6*d.* for baking, and 1*d.* for charcoal to keep the pies hot in the streets. Hence the capital required would be about 2*l.* in all.

A Balloon Flight

We had seen the Great Metropolis under almost every aspect. We had dived into the holes and corners hidden from the honest and well-to-do portion of the London community. We had visited Jacob's Island (the plague-spot of the British Capital) in the height of the cholera, when to inhale the very air of the place was to imbibe the breath of death. We had sought out the haunts of beggars and thieves, and passed hours communing with them as to their histories, habits, thoughts, and impulses. We had examined the World of London below the moral surface, as it were; and we had a craving, like the rest of mankind, to contemplate it from above; so, being offered a seat in the car of the Royal Nassau Balloon, we determined upon accompanying Mr Green into the clouds on his five hundredth ascent.

It was late in the evening (a fine autumn one) when the gun was fired that was the signal for the great gas-bag to be loosened from the ropes that held it down to the soil; and, immediately the buoyant machine bounded, like a big ball, into the air. Or, rather let us say, the earth seemed to sink suddenly down, as if the spot of ground to which it had been previously fastened had been constructed upon the same principle as the Adelphi stage, and admitted of being lowered at a moment's notice. Indeed, no sooner did the report of the gun clatter in the air, than the people, who had before been grouped about the car, appeared to fall from a level with the eye; and, instantaneously, there was seen a multitude of flat, upturned faces in the gardens below, with a dense *chevaux de frise* of arms extended above them, and some hundreds of outstretched hands fluttering farewell to us.

The moment after this, the balloon vaulted over the trees, and we saw the roadway outside the gardens stuck all over with mobs of little black Lilliputian people, while the hubbub of the voices below, and the cries of 'Ah *bal*-loon!' from the boys, rose to the ear like the sound of a distant school let loose to play.

Now began that peculiar panoramic effect which is the distinguishing feature of the first portion of a view from a balloon, and which arises from the utter absence of all sense of motion in the machine itself, and the consequent transference of the movement to the ground beneath. The earth, as the aeronautic vessel glided over it, seemed positively to consist of a continuous series of scenes which were being drawn along underneath us, as if it were some diorama laid flat upon the ground, and almost gave one the notion that the world was an endless landscape stretched upon rollers, which some invisible sprites below were busy revolving for our especial amusement.

Then, as we floated along, above the fields in a line with the Thames towards Richmond, and looked over the edge of the car in which we were standing (and which, by the bye, was like a big 'buck-basket,' reaching to one's breast), the sight was the most exquisite visual delight ever experienced. The houses directly underneath us looked like the tiny wooden things out of a child's box of toys, and the streets as if they were ruts in the ground; and we could hear the hum of the voices rising from every spot we passed over, faint as the buzzing of so many bees.

Far beneath, in the direction we were sailing, lay the suburban fields; and here the earth, with its tiny hills and plains and streams, assumed the appearance of the little coloured plaster models of countries. The roadways striping the land were like narrow brown ribbons, and the river, which we could see winding far away, resembled a long, gray, metallic-looking snake, creeping through the fields. The bridges over the Thames were positively like planks; and the tiny black barges, as they floated along the stream, seemed no bigger than summer insects on the water. The largest meadows were about the size of green-baize table covers; and across these we could just trace the line of the South-Western Railway, with the little whiff of white steam issuing from some passing engine, and no greater in volume than the jet of vapour from an ordinary tea-kettle.

Then, as the dusk of evening approached, and the gas-lights along the different lines of road started into light, one after another, the ground seemed to be covered with little illumination lamps, such as are hung on Christmas-trees, and reminding one of those that are occasionally placed, at intervals, along the grass at the edge of the gravel-walks in suburban tea-gardens; whilst the clusters of little lights at the spots where the hamlets were scattered over the scene, appeared like a knot of fire-flies in the air; and in the midst of these the eye could, here and there, distinguish the tiny crimson speck of some railway signal.

In the opposite direction to that in which the wind was insensibly wafting the balloon, lay the leviathan Metropolis, with a dense canopy of smoke hanging over it, and reminding one of the fog of vapour that is often seen steaming up from the fields at early morning. It was impossible to tell where the monster city began or ended, for the buildings stretched not only to the horizon on either side, but far away into thc distancc, whcrc, owing to thc coming shades of evening and the dense fumes from the million chimneys, the town seemed to blend into the sky, so that there was no distinguishing earth from heaven. The multitude of roofs that extended back from the foreground was positively like a dingy red sea, heaving in bricken billows, and the seeming wavcs rising up onc aftcr the other till the eye grew wearied with following them. Here and there we could distinguish little bare green patches of parks, and occasionally make out the tiny circular enclosures of the principal squares, though, from the height, these appeared scarcely bigger than wafers. Further, the fog of smoke that over-shadowed the giant town was pierced with a thousand steeples and pin-like factory-chimncys.

That little building, no bigger than one of the small china houscs that arc uscd for burning pastilles in, is Buckingham Palace – with St James's Park, dwindled to the size of a card-table, stretched out before it. Yonder is Bethlehem Hospital, with its dome, now of about the same dimensions as a bell.

Then the little mites of men, crossing the bridges, seemed to have no more motion in them than the animalcules in cheese; while the streets appeared more like cracks in the soil than highways, and the tiny steamers on the river were only to be distinguished by the thin black thread of smoke trailing after them.

Indeed, it was a most wonderful sight to behold that vast bricken mass of churches and hospitals, banks and prisons, palaces and workhouses, docks and refuges for the destitute, parks and squares, and courts and alleys, which make up London – all blent into one immense black spot – to look down upon the whole as the birds of the air look down upon it, and see it dwindled into a mere rubbish heap – to contemplate from afar that strange conglomeration of vice, avarice, and low cunning, of noble aspirations and humble heroism, and to grasp it in the eye, in all its incongruous integrity, at one single glance – to take, as it were, an angel's view of that huge town where, perhaps, there is more virtue and more iniquity, more wealth and more want, brought together into one dense focus than in any other part of the earth – to hear the hubbub of the restless sea of life and emotion below, and hear it, like the ocean in a shell, whispering of the incessant stragglings and chafings of the distant tide – to swing in the air high above all the petty jealousies and heart-burnings, small ambitions and vain parade of 'polite' society, and feel, for once, tranquil as a babe in a cot, and that you are hardly of the earth earthy, as, Jacob-like, you mount the aerial ladder, and half lose sight of the 'great commercial world' beneath, where men are regarded as mere counters to play with, and where to do your neighbour as your neighbour would do you constitutes the first principle in the religion of trade – to feel yourself floating through the endless realms of space, and drinking in the pure thin air of the skies, as you go sailing along almost among the stars, free as 'the lark at heaven's gate,' and enjoying, for a brief half hour, at least, a foretaste of that Elysian destiny which is the ultimate hope of all.

Such is the scene we behold, and such the thoughts that stir the brain on contemplating London from the car of a balloon.

The London Street Markets on a Saturday Night

The street-sellers are to be seen in the greatest numbers at the London street markets on a Saturday night. Here, and in the shops immediately adjoining, the working-classes generally purchase their Sunday's dinner; and after pay-time on Saturday night, or early on Sunday morning, the crowd in the New-cut, and the Brill in particular, is almost impassable. Indeed, the scene in these parts has more of the character of a fair than a market. There are hundreds of stalls, and every stall has its one or two lights; either it is illuminated by the intense white light of the new self-generating gas-lamp, or else it is brightened up by the red smoky flame of the old-fashioned grease lamps. One man shows off his yellow haddock with a candle stuck in a bundle of firewood; his neighbour makes a candlestick of a huge turnip, and the tallow gutters over its sides; whilst the boy shouting 'Eight a penny, stunning pears!' has rolled his dip in a thick coat of brown paper, that flares away with the candle. Some stalls are crimson with the fire shining through the holes beneath the baked-chestnut stove; others have handsome octahedral lamps, while a few have a candle shining through a sieve; these, with the sparkling ground-glass globes of the tea-dealers' shops, and the butchers' gaslights streaming and fluttering in the wind, like flags of flame, pour forth such a flood of light, that at a distance the atmosphere immediately above the spot is as lurid as if the pavement were on fire.

The pavement and the road are crowded with purchasers and street-sellers. The housewife in her thick shawl, with the market-basket on her arm, walks slowly on, stopping now to look at the stall of caps, and now to cheapen a bunch of greens. Little boys, holding three or four onions in their hand, creep between the people, wriggling their way through every interstice, and asking for custom in whining tones, as if seeking charity. Then the tumult of the thousand different cries of the eager dealers, all shouting at the top of their voices, at one and the same time, is almost bewildering. 'So-old again,' roars one. 'Chestnuts all 'ot, a penny a score,' bawls another. 'An 'aypenny a skin, blacking,' squeaks a boy. 'Buy, buy, buy, buy, buy – bu-u-uy!' cries the butcher. 'Half-quire of paper for a penny,' bellows the street stationer. 'An 'aypenny a lot ing-uns.' 'Twopence a pound grapes.' 'Three a penny Yarmouth bloaters.' 'Who'll buy a bonnet for fourpence?' 'Pick 'em out cheap here! Three pair for a halfpenny, bootlaces.' 'Now's your time! Beautiful whelks, a penny a lot.' 'Here's ha'p'orths,' shouts the perambulating confectioner. 'Come and look at 'em! Here's toasters!' bellows one with a Yarmouth bloater stuck on a toasting fork. 'Penny a lot, fine russets,' calls the apple woman: and so the Babel goes on.

One man stands with his red-edged mats hanging over his back and chest, like a herald's coat; and the girl with her basket of walnuts lifts her brown-stained fingers to her mouth, as she screams, 'Fine warnuts! Sixteen a penny, fine war-r-nuts.' A bootmaker, to 'ensure custom,' has illuminated his shop-front with a line of gas, and in its full glare stands a blind beggar, his eyes turned up so as to show only 'the whites,' and mumbling some begging rhymes, that are drowned in the shrill notes of the bamboo-flute-player next to him. The boy's sharp cry, the woman's cracked voice, the gruff, hoarse shout of the man, are all mingled together. Sometimes an Irishman is heard with his 'fine eating apples;' or else the jingling music of an unseen organ breaks out, as the trio of street singers rest between the verses.

Then the sights, as you elbow your way through the crowd, are equally multifarious. Here is a stall glittering with new tin saucepans; there another, bright with its blue and yellow crockery, and sparkling with white glass. Now you come to a row of old shoes arranged along the pavement; now to a stand of gaudy tea-trays; then to a shop with red handkerchiefs and blue checked shirts, fluttering backwards and forwards, and a counter built up outside on the kerb, beside which are boys beseeching custom. At the door of a tea-shop, with its hundred white globes of light, stands a man delivering bills, thanking the public for past favours, and 'defying competition.' Here, alongside the road, are some half-dozen headless tailors' dummies, dressed in Chesterfields and fustian jackets, each labelled, 'Look at the prices,' or 'Observe the quality.' After this a butcher's shop, crimson and white with meat piled up to the first-floor, in front of which the butcher himself, in his blue coat, walks up and down, sharpening his knife on the steel that hangs to his waist. A little further on stands the clean family, begging; the father with his head down as if in shame, and a box of lucifers held forth in his hand – the boys in newly-washed pinafores, and the tidily got-up mother with a child at her breast. This stall is green and white with bunches of turnips – that red with apples, the next yellow with onions, and another purple with pickling cabbages. One minute you pass a man with an umbrella turned inside up and full of prints; the next, you hear one with a peep show of Mazeppa, and Paul Jones the pirate, describing the pictures to the boys looking in at the little round windows. Then is heard the sharp snap of the percussion-cap from the crowd of lads firing at the target for nuts; and the moment afterwards, you see either a black man half-clad in white, and shivering in the cold with tracts in his hand, or else you hear the sounds of music from 'Frazier's Circus,' on the other side of the road, and the man outside the door of the penny concert, beseeching you to 'Be in time – be in time!' as Mr Somebody is just about to sing his favourite song of the 'Knife Grinder.' Such, indeed, is the riot, the struggle, and the scramble for a living, that the confusion and uproar of the New-Cut on Saturday night have a bewildering and saddening effect upon the thoughtful mind.

Each salesman tries his utmost to sell his wares, tempting the passers-by with his bargains. The boy with his stock of herbs offers 'a double 'andful of fine parsley for a penny;' the man with the donkey-cart filled with turnips has three lads to shout for him to their utmost, with their 'Ho! ho! hi-i-i! What do you think of this here? A penny a bunch – hurrah for free trade! *Here's* your turnips!' Until it is seen and heard, we have no sense of the scramble that is going on throughout London for a living. The same scene takes place at the Brill – the same in Leather Lane – the same in

Tottenham-court-road – the same in Whitecross-street; go to whatever corner of the metropolis you please, either on a Saturday night or a Sunday morning, and there is the same shouting and the same struggling to get the penny profit out of the poor man's Sunday's dinner.

Since the above description was written the New-Cut has lost much of its noisy and brilliant glory. In consequence of a New Police regulation, 'stands' or 'pitches' have been forbidden, and each coster, on a market night, is now obliged, under pain of the lock-up house, to carry his tray, or keep moving with his barrow. The gay stalls have been replaced by deal boards, some sodden with wet fish, others stained purple with blackberries, or brown with walnut-peel; and the bright lamps are almost totally superseded by the dim, guttering candle. Even if the pole under the tray or 'shallow' is seen resting on the ground, the policeman on duty is obliged to interfere.

The mob of purchasers has diminished one-half; and instead of the road being filled with customers and trucks, the pavements and kerbstones are scarcely crowded.

Of the 'Penny Gaff'

In many of the thoroughfares of London there are shops which have been turned into a kind of temporary theatre (admission one penny), where dancing and singing take place every night. Rude pictures of the performers are arranged outside, to give the front a gaudy and attractive look, and at night-time coloured lamps and transparencies are displayed to draw an audience. These places are called by the costers 'Penny Gaffs;' and on a Monday night as many as six performances will take place, each one having its two hundred visitors . . .

The 'penny gaff' chosen was situated in a broad street near Smithfield; and for a great distance off, the jingling sound of music was heard, and the gas-light streamed out into the thick night air as from a dark lantern, glittering on the windows of the houses opposite, and lighting up the faces of the mob in the road, as on an illumination night. The front of a large shop had been entirely removed, and the entrance was decorated with paintings of the 'comic singers,' in their most 'humorous' attitudes. On a table against the wall was perched the band, playing what the costers call 'dancing tunes' with great effect, for the hole at the money-takers box was blocked up with hands tendering the penny. The crowd without was so numerous, that a policeman was in attendance to preserve order, and push the boys off the pavement – the music having the effect of drawing them insensibly towards the festooned green-baize curtain.

The shop itself had been turned into a waiting-room, and was crowded even to the top of the stairs leading to the gallery on the first floor. The ceiling of this 'lobby' was painted blue, and spotted with whitewash clouds, to represent the heavens; the boards of the trapdoor, and the laths that showed through the holes in the plaster, being all of the same colour. A notice was here posted, over the canvass door leading into the theatre, to the effect that 'Ladies and Gentlemen to the Front Places must pay Twopence.'

The visitors, with few exceptions, were all boys and girls, whose ages seemed to vary from eight to twenty years. Some of the girls – though their figures showed them to be mere children – were dressed in showy cotton-velvet polkas, and wore dowdy feathers in their crushed bonnets. They stood laughing and joking with the lads, in an unconcerned, impudent manner, that was almost appalling. Some of them, when tired of waiting, chose their partners, and commenced dancing grotesquely, to the admiration of the lookers-on, who expressed their approbation in obscene terms, that, far from disgusting the poor little women, were received as compliments, and acknowledged with smiles and coarse repartees. The boys clustered together, smoking their pipes, and laughing at each other's anecdotes, or else jingling halfpence in time with the tune, while they whistled an accompaniment to it. Presently one of the performers, with a gilt crown on his well-greased locks, descended from the staircase, his fleshings covered by a dingy dressing-gown, and mixed with the mob, shaking hands with old acquaintances. The 'comic singer,' too, made his appearance among the throng – the huge bow to his cravat, which nearly covered his waistcoat, and the red end to his nose, exciting neither merriment nor surprise.

To discover the kind of entertainment, a lad near me and my companion was asked 'if there was any flash dancing.' With a knowing wink the boy answered, 'Lots! Show their legs and all, prime!' and immediately the boy followed up his information by a request for a 'yennep' to get a 'tib of occabot.' After waiting in the lobby some considerable time, the performance inside was concluded, and the audience came pouring out through the canvass door. As they had to pass singly, I noticed them particularly. Above three-fourths of them were women and girls, the rest consisting chiefly of mere boys – for out of about two hundred persons I counted only eighteen men. Forward they came, bringing an overpowering stench with them, laughing and yelling as they pushed their way through the waiting-room. One woman carrying a sickly child with a bulging forehead, was reeling drunk, the saliva running down her mouth as she stared about her with a heavy fixed eye. Two boys were pushing her from side to side, while the poor infant slept, breathing heavily, as if stupefied, through the din. Lads jumping on girls' shoulders, and girls laughing hysterically from being tickled by the youths behind them, everyone shouting and jumping, presented a mad scene of frightful enjoyment.

When these had left, a rush for places by those in waiting began, that set at defiance the blows and strugglings of a lady in spangles who endeavoured to preserve order and take the checks. As time was a great object with the proprietor, the entertainment within began directly the first seat was taken, so that the lads without, rendered furious by the rattling of the piano within, made the canvas partition bulge in and out, with the struggling of those seeking admission, like a sail in a flagging wind.

To form the theatre, the first floor had been removed; the whitewashed beams however still stretched from wall to wall. The lower room had evidently been the warehouse, while the upper apartment had been the sitting-room, for the paper was still on the walls. A gallery, with a canvas front, had been hurriedly built up, and it was so fragile that the boards bent under the weight of those above. The bricks in the warehouse were smeared over with red paint, and had a few black curtains daubed upon them. The coster-youths require no very great scenic embellishment, and indeed the stage – which was about eight feet square – could admit of none. Two jets of gas, like those outside a butcher's shop, were placed on each side of the proscenium, and proved very handy for the gentlemen whose pipes required lighting. The band inside the 'theatre' could not compare with the band without. An old grand piano, whose canvas-covered top extended the entire length of the stage, sent forth its wiry notes under the be-ringed fingers of a 'professor Wilkinsini,' while another professional, with his head resting on his violin, played vigorously, as he stared unconcernedly at the noisy audience.

Singing and dancing formed the whole of the hour's performance, and, of the two, the singing was preferred. A young girl, of about fourteen years of age, danced with more energy than grace, and seemed to be well-known to the spectators, who cheered her on by her Christian name. When the dance was concluded, the proprietor of the establishment threw down a penny from the gallery, in the hopes that others might be moved to similar acts of generosity; but no one followed up the offer, so the young lady hunted after the money and departed. The 'comic singer,' in a battered hat and the huge bow to his cravat, was received with deafening shouts. Several songs were named by the costers, but the 'funny gentleman' merely requested them 'to hold their jaws,' and putting on a 'knowing' look, sang a song, the whole point of which consisted in the mere utterance of some filthy word at the end of each stanza. Nothing, however, could have been more successful. The lads stamped their feet with delight; the girls screamed with enjoyment. Once or twice a young shrill laugh would anticipate the fun – as if the words were well known – or the boys would forestall the point by shouting it out before the proper time. When the song was ended the house was in a delirium of applause. The canvas front to the gallery was beaten with sticks, drum-like, and sent down showers of white powder on the heads in the pit. Another song followed, and the actor knowing on what his success depended, lost no opportunity of increasing his laurels. The most obscene thoughts, the most disgusting scenes were coolly described, making a poor child near me wipe away the tears that rolled down her eyes with the enjoyment of the poison. There were three or four of these songs sung during the course of the evening, each one being encored, and then changed. One written about 'Pine-apple rock,' was the grand treat of the night, and offered greater scope to the rhyming powers of the author than any of the others. In this, not a single chance had been missed; ingenuity had been exerted to its utmost lest an obscene thought should be passed by, and it was absolutely awful to behold the relish with which the young ones jumped to the hideous meaning of the verses.

There was one scene yet to come that was perfect in its wickedness. A ballet began between a man dressed up as a woman, and a country clown. The most disgusting attitudes were struck, the most immoral acts represented, without one dissenting voice. If there had been any feat of agility, any grimacing, or, in fact, anything with which the laughter of the uneducated classes is usually associated, the applause might have been accounted for; but here were two ruffians degrading themselves each time they stirred a limb, and forcing into the brains of the childish audience before them thoughts that must embitter a lifetime, and descend from father to child like some bodily infirmity.

The Port of London

Seen from the Custom House, this is indeed a characteristic sight; and some time since we were permitted, by the courtesy of the authorities, to witness the view from the 'long room' there.

The broad highway of the river – which at this part is near upon 300 yards in width – was almost blocked with the tiers of shipping; for there was merely a narrow pathway of grey, glittering water left open in the middle; and, on either side, the river was black with the dense mass of hulls collected alongside the quays; while the masts of the craft were as thick as the pine stems in their native forests.

The sun shone bright upon the water, and as its broken beams played upon the surface it sparkled and twinkled in the light, like a crumpled plate of golden foil; and down the 'silent highway,' barges, tide-borne, floated sideways, with their long slim oars projecting from their sides like the fins of a flying fish; whilst others went along, with their masts slanting down and their windlass clicking as men laboured to raise the 'warm-brown ' sail that they had lowered to pass under the bridge. Then came a raft of timber, towed by a small boat, and the boatman leaning far back in it as he tugged at the sculls; and presently a rapid river steamer flitted past, the deck crowded so densely with passengers that it reminded one of a cushion stuck all over with black pins;

and as it hurried past we caught a whiff, as it were, of music from the little band on board.

The large square blocks of warehouses on the opposite shore were almost hidden in the shadow which came slanting down far into the river, and covering, as with a thick veil of haze, the confused knot of sloops and schooners and 'bilanders' that lay there in the dusk, in front of the wharves. Over the tops of the warehouses we could see the trail of white steam, from the railway engines at the neighbouring terminus, darting from among the roofs as they hurried to and fro.

A little way down the river, stood a clump of Irish vessels, with the light peeping through the thicket, as it were, of their masts – some with their sails hanging all loose and limp, and others with them looped in rude festoons to the yards. Beside these lay barges stowed full of barrels of beer and sacks of flour; and a few yards farther on, a huge foreign steamer appeared, with short thick black funnel and blue paddle-boxes. Then came hoys laden with straw and coasting goods, and sunk so deep in the water that, as the steamers dashed by, the white spray was seen to beat against the dark tarpaulins that covered their heaped-up cargoes. Next to these the black, surly-looking colliers were noted, huddled in a dense mass together, with the bare backs of the coalwhippers flashing among the rigging as, in hoisting the 'Wallsend' from the hold, they leaped at intervals down upon the deck.

Behind, and through the tangled skeins of the rigging, the eye rested upon the old Suffranco wharves, with their peaked roofs and unwieldy cranes; and far at the back we caught sight of one solitary tree; whilst in the fog of the extreme distance the steeple of St Mary's, Rotherhithe, loomed over the mast-heads – grey, dim, and spectral-like.

Then, as we turned round and looked towards the bridge, we caught glimpses of barges and boats moving in the broad arcs of light showing through the arches; while above the bridge-parapet were seen just the tops of moving carts, and omnibuses, and high-loaded railway wagons, hurrying along in opposite directions.

Glancing thence to the bridge-wharves on the same side of the river as ourselves, we beheld bales of goods dangling in the air from the cranes that projected from the top of 'Nicholson's.' Here alongside the quay lay Spanish schooners and brigs, laden with fruits; and as we cast our eye below, we saw puppet-like figures of men with cases of oranges on their backs, bending beneath the load, on their way across the dumb-lighter to the wharf.

Next came Billingsgate, and here we could see the white bellies of the fish showing in the market beneath, and streams of men passing backwards and forwards to the river side, where lay a small crowd of Dutch eel boats, with their gutta-percha-like hulls, and unwieldy, green-tipped rudders. Immediately beneath us was the brown, gravelled walk of the Custom House quay, where trim children strolled with their nursemaids, and hatless and yellow-legged Blue-coat Boys, and there were youths fresh from school, who had come either to have a peep at the shipping, or to skip and play among the barges.

From the neighbouring stairs boats pushed off continually, while men standing in the stern wriggled themselves along by working a scull behind, after the fashion of a fish's tail.

Here, near the front of the quay, lay a tier of huge steamers with gilt sterns and mahogany wheels, and their bright brass binnacles shining as if on fire in the sun. At the foremast head of one of these the 'blue Peter' was flying as a summons to the hands on shore to come aboard, while the dense clouds of smoke that poured from the thick red funnel told that the boiler fires were ready lighted for starting.

Further on, might be seen the old 'Perseus,' the receiving-ship of the navy, with her topmasts down, her black sides towering high, like immense rampart-walls, out of the water, and her long white ventilating sacks hanging over the hatchways. Immediately beyond this, the eye could trace the Tower wharves, with their gravelled walks, and the high-capped and red-coated sentry pacing up and down them, and the square old grey lump of the Tower, with a turret at each of its four corners, peering over the water. In front of this lay another dense crowd of foreign vessels, and with huge lighters beside the wharf, while bales of hemp and crates of hardware swung from the cranes as they were lowered into the craft below.

In the distance, towered the huge massive warehouses of St Katherine's Dock, with their big signet letters on their sides, their many prison-like windows, and their cranes and doors to every floor. Beyond this, the view was barred out by the dense grove of masts that rose up from the water, thick as giant reeds beside the shore, and filmed over with the grey mist of vapour rising from the river so that their softened outlines melted gently into the dusk.

As we stood looking down upon the river, the hundred clocks of the hundred churches at our back, with the golden figures on their black dials shining in the sun, chimed the hour of noon, and in a hundred different tones; while solemnly above all boomed forth the deep metallic moan of St Paul's; and scarcely had the great bell ceased humming in the air, before there rose the sharp tinkling of eight bells from the decks of the multitude of sailing vessels and steamers packed below.

Indeed, there was an exquisite charm in the many different sounds that smote the ear from the busy Port of London. Now we could hear the ringing of the 'purlman's' bell, as, in his little boat, he flitted in and out among the several tiers of colliers to serve the grimy and half-naked coalwhippers with drink. Then would come the rattle of some heavy chain suddenly let go, and after this the chorus of many seamen heaving at the ropes; whilst high above all roared the hoarse voice of someone on the shore, bawling through his hands to a mate aboard the craft. Presently came the clicking of the capstan-palls, telling of the heaving of a neighbouring anchor; and mingling with all this might be heard the rumbling of the wagons and carts in the streets behind, and the panting and throbbing of the passing river steamers in front, together with the shrill scream of the railway whistle from the terminus on the opposite shore.

In fine, look or listen in whatever direction we might, the many sights and sounds that filled the eye and ear told each its different tale of busy trade, bold enterprise, and boundless capital. In the many bright-coloured flags that fluttered from the mastheads of the vessels crowding the port, we could read how all the corners of the earth had been ransacked each for its peculiar produce. The massive warehouses at the water-side looked really like the storehouses of the world's infinite products, and the tall mast-like factory chimneys behind us, with their black plumes of smoke streaming from them, told us how all around that port were hard at work fashioning the products into cunning fabrics.

Then, as we beheld the white clouds of steam from some passing railway engine puffed out once more from among the opposite roofs, and heard the clatter of the thousand vehicles in the streets hard by, and watched the dark tide of carts and wagons pouring over the bridge, and looked down the apparently endless vista of masts that crowded either side of the river – we could not help feeling how every power known to man was here used to bring and diffuse the riches of all parts of the world over our own, and indeed every other country.

Of Two Orphan Flower Girls

Of flower girls there are two classes. Some girls, and they are certainly the smaller class of the two, avail themselves of the sale of flowers in the streets for immoral purposes, or rather, they seek to eke out the small gains of their trade by such practices. They frequent the great thoroughfares, and offer their bouquets to gentlemen, whom on an evening they pursue for a hundred yards or two in such places as the Strand, mixing up a leer with their whine for custom or for charity. Their ages are from fourteen to nineteen or twenty, and sometimes they remain out offering their flowers – or dried lavender when no flowers are to be had – until late at night. They do not care, to make their appearance in the streets until towards evening, and though they solicit the custom of ladies, they rarely follow or importune them. Of this class I shall treat more fully under another head.

The other class of flower-girls is composed of the girls who, wholly or partially, depend upon the sale of flowers for their own support or as an assistance to their parents. Some of them are the children of street-sellers, some are orphans, and some are the daughters of mechanics who are out of employment, and who prefer any course rather than an application to the parish. These girls offer their flowers in the principal streets at the West End, and resort greatly to the suburbs; there are a few, also, in the business thoroughfares.

They walk up and down in front of the houses, offering their flowers to anyone looking out of the windows, or they stand at any likely place. They are generally very persevering, more especially the younger children, who will run along barefooted, with their 'Please, gentleman, do buy my flowers. Poor little girl!' – 'Please, kind lady, buy my violets. O, do! please! Poor little girl! Do buy a bunch, please, kind lady!'

The statement I give, 'of two orphan flower sellers' furnishes another proof, in addition to the many I have already given, of the heroic struggles of the poor, and of the truth of the saying 'What would the poor do without the poor?'

The better class of flower-girls reside in Lisson-grove, in the streets off Drury-lane, in St Giles's, and in other parts inhabited by the very poor. Some of them live in lodging-houses, the stench and squalor of which are in remarkable contrast to the beauty and fragrance of the flowers they sometimes have to carry thither with them unsold.

Of these girls the elder was fifteen and the younger eleven. Both were clad in old, but not torn, dark print frocks, hanging so closely, and yet so loosely, about them as to show the deficiency of underclothing; they wore old broken black chip bonnets. The older sister (or rather half-sister) had a pair of old worn-out shoes on her feet, the younger was barefoot, but trotted along, in a gait at once quick and feeble – as if the soles of her little feet were impervious, like horn, to the roughness of the road. The elder girl had a modest expression of countenance, with no pretensions to prettiness except in having tolerably good eyes. Her complexion was somewhat muddy, and her features somewhat pinched. The younger child had a round, chubby, and even rosy face, and quite a healthful look. [. . .]

They lived in one of the streets near Drury-lane. They were inmates of a house, not let out as a lodging house, in separate beds, but in rooms, and inhabited by street-sellers and street-labourers. The room they occupied was large, and one dim candle lighted it so insufficiently that it seemed to exaggerate the dimensions. The walls were bare and discoloured with damp. The furniture consisted of a crazy table and a few chairs, and in the centre of the room was an old four-post bedstead of the larger size. This bed was occupied nightly by the two sisters and their brother, a lad just turned thirteen. In a sort of recess in a corner of the room was the decency of an old curtain – or something equivalent, for I could hardly see in the dimness – and behind this was, I presume, the bed of the married couple. The three children paid 2*s.* a week for the room, the tenant an Irishman out of work paying 2*s.* 9*d.*, but the furniture was his, and his wife aided the children in their trifle of washing, mended their clothes, where such a thing was possible, and such like. The husband was absent at the time of my visit, but the wife seemed of a better stamp, judging by her appearance, and by her refraining from any direct, or even indirect, way of begging, as well as from the 'Glory be to Gods!' 'the heavens be your honour's bed!' or 'it's the thruth I'm telling of you sire,' that I so frequently meet with on similar visits.

The elder girl said, in an English accent, not at all garrulously, but merely in answer to my questions: 'I sell flowers, sir; we live almost on flowers when they are to be got. I sell, and so does my sister, all kinds, but it's very little use offering any that's not sweet. I think it's the sweetness as sells them. I sell primroses, when they're in, and violets, and wall-flowers, and stocks, and roses of different sorts, and pinks, and carnations, and mixed flowers, and lilies of the valley, and green lavender, and mignonette (but that I do very seldom), and violets again at this time of the year, for we get them both in spring and winter.' [They are forced in hot-houses for winter sale, I may remark.] 'The best sale of all is, I think, moss-roses, young moss-roses. We do best of all on them. Primroses are good, for people say: "Well, here's spring again to a certainty." Gentlemen are our best customers. I've heard that they buy flowers to give to the ladies. Ladies have sometimes said: "A penny, my poor girl, here's three-halfpence for the bunch." Or they've given me the price of two bunches for one; so have gentlemen. I never had a rude word said to me by a gentleman in my life. No, sir, neither lady nor gentleman ever gave me 6*d*. for a bunch of flowers. I never had a sixpence given to me in my life – never. I never go among boys, I know nobody but my brother. My father was a tradesman in Mitchelstown, in the County Cork. I don't know what sort of a tradesman he was. I never saw him. He was a tradesman I've been told. I was born in London. Mother was a chairwoman, and lived very well. None of us ever saw a father.' [It was evident that they were illegitimate children, but the landlady had never seen the mother, and could give me no information.] 'We don't know anything about our fathers. We were all "mother's children." Mother died seven years ago last Guy Faux day. I've got myself, and my brother and sister a bit of bread ever since, and never had any help but from the neighbours. I never troubled the parish. O, yes, sir, the neighbours is all poor people, very poor, some of them. We've lived with her' (indicating her landlady by a gesture) 'these two years, and off and on before that. I can't say how long.' 'Well, I don't know exactly,' said the landlady, 'but I've had them with me almost all the time, for four years, as near as I can recollect; perhaps more. I've moved three times, and they always followed me.' In answer to my inquiries the landlady assured me that these two poor girls, were never out of doors all the time she had known them after six at night. 'We've always good health. We can all read.' [Here the three somewhat insisted upon proving to me their proficiency in reading, and having produced a Roman Catholic book, the 'Garden of Heaven,' they read very well.] 'I put myself,' continued the girl, 'and I put my brother and sister to a Roman Catholic school – and to Ragged schools – but I could read before mother died. My brother can write, and I pray to God that he'll do well with it. I buy my flowers at Convent Garden; sometimes, but very seldom, at Farringdon. I pay 1*s*. for a dozen bunches, whatever flowers are in. Out of every two bunches I can make three, at 1*d*. a piece. Sometimes one or two over in the dozen, but not so often as I would like. We make the bunches up ourselves. We get the rush to tie them with for nothing. We put their own leaves round these violets (she produced a bunch). The paper for a dozen costs a penny; sometimes only a halfpenny. The two of us doesn't make less than 6*d*. a day, unless it's very ill luck. But religion teaches us that God will support us, and if we make less we say nothing. We do better on oranges in March or April, I think it is, than on flowers. Oranges keep better than flowers, you see, sir. We make 1*s*.

a day, and 9*d*. a day, on oranges, the two of us. I wish they was in all the year. I generally go St John's-wood way, and Hampstead and Highgate way with my flowers. I can get them nearly all the year, but oranges is better liked than flowers, I think. I always keep 1*s*. stock-money if I can. If it's bad weather, so bad that we can't sell flowers at all, and so if we've had to spend our stock-money for a bit of bread, *she* (the landlady) lends us 1*s*., if she has one, or she borrows one of a neighbour, if she hasn't, or if the neighbours hasn't it, she borrows it at a dolly shop' [the illegal pawnshop]. 'There's 2*d*. a week to pay for 1*s*. at a dolly, and perhaps an old rug left for it; if it's very hard weather, the rug must be taken at night time, or we are starved with the cold. It sometimes has to be put into the dolly again next morning, and then there's 2*d*. to pay for it for the day. We've had a frock in for 6*d*., and that's a penny a week, and the same for a day. We never pawned anything; we have nothing they would take in at the pawnshop. We live on bread and tea, and sometimes a fresh herring of a night. Sometimes we don't eat a bit all day when we're out; sometimes we take a bit of bread with us, or buy a bit. My sisters can't eat taturs; they sicken her. I don't know what emigrating means.' [I informed her and she continued]: 'No, sir, I wouldn't like to emigrate and leave brother and sister. If they went with me I don't think I should like it, not among strangers. I think our living costs us 2*s*. a week for the two of us; the rest goes in rent. That's all we make.'

The brother earned from 1*s*. 6*d*. to 2*s*. a week, with an occasional meal, as a costermonger's boy. Neither of them ever missed mass on a Sunday.

A Train to Clapham Common

The ascent of a mountain in the tropics, and gradual passage through the several atmospheric layers of different climates, reveals, as we rise above the plains, the mountain sides prismatically belted, as it were, with the rainbow hues of various zones of fruits and flowers – the same as if we had passed along rather than above the surface of the globe – from the brilliant and glowing tints of vegetable nature at the tropics, to the sombre shades of the hardier plants and trees peculiar to the colder regions, even till we ultimately reach, at the peak, the colourless desolation of the poles themselves. But this journeying upwards through the various botanical strata, as it were, of the earth is hardly more peculiar and marked than is the rapid transition now-a-days, while travelling on some London railway, from town to the country; for as we fly along the house-tops through the various suburban zones encircling the giant Metropolis, we can see the bricken city gradually melt away into the green fields, and the streets glide, like solid rivers, into the roads, and cabs and busses merge into wagons and ploughs, while factories give place to market-gardens, and parks and squares fade gradually into woods and corn-fields.

Perhaps this change, from civic to rustic scenery – this dissolving view, as it were, of the capital melting into the country, is nowhere better seen than in a half-hour's trip along the Southampton rail; for no sooner have we crossed the viaduct spanning the Westminster Road, and looked down upon the drivers at the back of the passing Hansoms, and the carters perched on the high box-seats of the railway-carriers' vans, as well as the passengers ranged along the roof of the Kennington omnibuses; and had a glimpse, moreover, at the bright-coloured rolls of carpets standing in the first-floor windows of the great linendrapery styled 'Lambeth House,' than we are whisked into the region of innumerable factories – the tall black chimneys piercing the air as thickly as the minarets of some Turkish city; and then, even with the eyes shut, the nose can tell, by the succession of chemical stenches assailing it, that we are being wafted through the several zones of Lambeth manufactures. Now we get a whiff of the gutta-percha works; then comes a faint gust from some floor-cloth shed; next we dash through an odoriferous belt of bone-boiling atmosphere; and after that through a film of fetor rank with the fumes from the glazing of the potteries; whereupon this is followed by bands of nauseous vapours from decomposing hides and horses' hoofs, resin and whiting works; and the next instant these give place to layer after layer of sickening exhalations from gas-factories, and soap-boiling establishments, and candle-companies; so that we are thus led by the nose along a chromatic scale, as it were, of the strong suburban stenches that encompass, in positive rings of nausea, the great cathedral dome of the Metropolis, like the phosphoric glory environing the head of some renowned Catholic saint.

Nor is the visional diorama that then glides past us less striking and characteristic than the nasal one. What a dense huddle and confused bricken crowd of houses and hovels does the city seem to be composed of; the very train itself appears to be ploughing its way through the walls of the houses, while each gable end that is turned towards the rail is used as a means to advertise the wares of some enterprising tradesman.

Now the cathedral-like dome of Bedlam flits before the eye, and now a huge announcement tells us that we are flying past the famed concert-tavern called Canterbury Hall. Then we catch just a glimpse of the green gardens and old ruby towers of Lambeth Palace; and no sooner has this whizzed by, and we have seen the river twinkle for a moment in the light, like a steel-plate flashing in the sun, than we are in the regions of the potteries, with their huge kilns, like enormous bricken skittles, and rows of yellow-looking pipes and pans ranged along the walls. The moment afterwards the gas-works, with their monster black iron drums, dart by the window of the carriage; and the next instant the old, gloomy, and desolate-looking Vauxhall Gardens, with its white rotunda, like a dingy twelfth-cake ornament, glides swiftly by. Then we have another momentary peep down into the road, and have hardly noted the monster railway taverns, and seen the small forest of factory chimneys here grouped about the bridge, with Price's gigantic candle-works hard by, than we are flying past the old Nine Elms station. No sooner has this flitted by than the scene is immediately shifted, and a small, muddy canal is beheld, skirted with willows; and then the tall metal syphon of the water-works, like a monster hair-pin stuck in the earth, shoots rapidly into sight; whereupon the view begins to open a bit, revealing

Chelsea Hospital, with its green copper roof and red and white front, on the other side of the river; while the crowd of dwellings grows suddenly less dense, and the houses and factories dwindle into cottages with small patches of garden. Here, too, the London streets end, and the highroads, the lanes, and hedges make their appearance; while large, flat fields of the suburban market-garden rush by, each scored with line after line of plants. Nor is it many minutes more before these vast plains of cabbage and tracts of potatoes are succeeded by a glance of sloping lawns and pleasant-looking country villas, ranged alongside the raised roadway; immediately after which we are in the land of railway cuttings, with the line sunk in a trough of deep green shelving banks, instead of being buried, as it was only a few minutes before, among the sloping roofs and chimney-pots of the smoky London houses.

Another instant, and the train rattles through a little tunnel, and then is heard the sharp, shrill scream of the whistle; whereupon porters dart by the carriage windows, crying, 'Clapham Common! Clapham Common!' and the instant afterwards are landed at the little rustic station there.

Of the Street-Sellers of Live Birds

The bird-sellers in the streets are also the bird-catchers in the fields, plains, heaths and woods, which still surround the metropolis; and in compliance with established precedent it may be proper that I should give an account of the catching, before I proceed to any further statement of the procedure subsequent thereunto . . .

It is principally effected by means of nets. A bird-net is about twelve yards square; it is spread flat upon the ground, to which it is secured by four 'stars.' These are iron pins, which are inserted in the field, and hold the net, but so that the two 'wings' or 'flaps', which are indeed the sides of the net, are not confined by the stars. In the middle of the net is a cage with a fine wire roof, widely worked, containing the 'call bird.' This bird is trained to sing loudly and cheerily, great care being bestowed upon its tuition, and its song attracts the wild birds. Sometimes a few stuffed birds are spread about the cage as if a flock were already assembling there. The bird-catcher lies flat and motionless on the ground, 20 or 30 yards distant from the edge of the net. As soon as he considers that a sufficiency of birds have congregated around his decoy, he rapidly draws towards him a line, called the 'pull-line' of which he has kept hold. This is so looped and run within the edges of the net, that on being smartly pulled, the two wings of the net collapse and fly together, the stars still keeping their hold, and the net encircles the cage of the call bird, and incloses in its folds all the wild birds allured round it. In fact it then resembles a great cage of network. The captives are secured in cages – the call-bird continuing to sing as if in mockery of their struggles – or in hampers proper for the purpose, which are carried on the man's back to London . . .

The bird-catcher's life has many, and to the constitution of some minds, irresistible charms. There is the excitement of 'sport' – not the headlong excitement of the chase, where the blood is stirred by motion and exercise – but still sport surpassing that of the angler, who plies his finest art to capture one fish at a time, while the bird-catcher despises an individual capture, but seeks to ensnare a flock at one twitch of the line. There is, moreover, the attraction of idleness, at least for intervals – perhaps the great charm of fishing – and basking in the lazy sunshine, to watch the progress of the snares. Birds, however, and more especially linnets, are caught in the winter, when it is not such quite holiday work. A bird-dealer (not a street dealer) told me that the greatest number of birds he had ever heard of as having been caught at one pull was nearly 200. My informant happened to be present on the occasion. 'Pulls' of 50, 100, and 150 are not very unfrequent when the young broods are all on the wing.

Of the bird-catchers, including all who reside in Woolwich, Greenwich, Hounslow, Isleworth, Barnet, Uxbridge, and places of similar distance, all working for the London market, there are about 200. The localities where these men 'catch', are the neighbourhoods of the places I have mentioned as their residences, and at Holloway, Hampstead,

Highgate, Finchley, Battersea, Blackheath, Putney, Mortlake, Chiswick, Richmond, Hampton, Kingston, Eltham, Carshalton, Streatham, the Tootings, Woodford, Epping, Snaresbrook, Walthamstow, Tottenham, Edmonton – wherever, in fine, are open fields, plains or commons around the metropolis . . .

A young man, rather tall, and evidently active, but very thin, gave me the following account. His manners were quiet and his voice low. His dress could not so well be called mean as hard worn, with the unmistakable look of much of the attire of his class, that it was not made for the wearer; his surtout, for instance, which was fastened in front by two buttons, reached down to his ancles, and could have enclosed a bigger man. He resided in St Luke's, in which parish there are more bird-catchers living than in any other. A heavy old sofa, in the well of which was a bed, a table, two chairs, a fender, a small closet containing a few pots and tins, and some twenty empty bird-cages of different sizes hung against the walls. In a sort of wooden loft, which had originally been constructed, he believed, for the breeding of fancy-pigeons, and which was erected on the roof, were about a dozen or two of cages, some old and broken, and in them a few live goldfinches, which hopped about very merrily. They were all this year's birds, and my informant, who had 'a little connection of his own,' was rearing them in hopes they would turn out good specs, quite 'birds beyond the run of the streets.' The place and the cages, each bird having its own little cage, were very clean, but at the time of my visit the loft was exceedingly hot, as the day was one of the sultriest. Lest this heat should prove too great for the finches, the timbers on all sides were well wetted and re-wetted at intervals, for about an hour at noon, at which time only was the sun full on the loft.

'I shall soon have more birds, sir,' he said, 'but you see I only put aside here such as are the very best of the take; all cocks, of course. O, I've been in the trade all my life; I've had a turn at other things, certainly, but this life suits me best, I think, because I have my health best in it. My father – he's been dead a goodish bit – was a bird-catcher as well, and he used to take me out with him as soon as I was strong enough; when I was about ten I suppose. I don't remember my mother. Father was brought up to brick-making. I believe that most of the bird-catchers that have been trades, and that's not half, a quarter perhaps, were brick-makers, or something that way. Well, I don't know the reason. The brick-making was, in my father's young days, carried on more in the country, and the bird-catchers used to fall in with the brick-makers, and so perhaps that led to it. I've heard my father tell of an old soldier that had been discharged with a pension being the luckiest bird-catcher he knowed. The soldier was a bird-catcher before he first listed, and he listed drunk. I once – yes, sire, I dare say that's fifteen year back, for I was quite a lad – walked with my father and captain' [the pensioner's sobriquet] 'till they parted for work, and I remember very well I heard him tell how, when on march in Portingal – I think that's what he called it, but it's in foreign parts – he saw flocks of birds; he wished he could be after catching them, for he was well tired of sogering. I was sent to school twice or thrice, and can read a little and write a little; and I should like reading better if I could manage it better. I read a penny number, or "the police" in a newspaper, now and then, but very seldom. But on a fine day I hated being at school. I wanted to be at work, to make something at bird-catching. If a boy can make money, why shouldn't he? And if I'd had a net, or cage, and a mule of my own, then, I thought, I could make money.' [I may observe that the mule longed for by my informant was a 'cross' between two birds, and was wanted for the decoy. Some bird-catchers contend that a mule makes the best call-bird of any; others that the natural note of the linnet, for instance, was more alluring than the song of a mule between a linnet and a goldfinch. One birdman told me that the excellence of a mule was, that it had been bred and taught by its master, had never been at large, and was 'better to manage;' it was bolder, too, in a cage, and its notes were often loud and ringing, and might be heard to a considerable distance.]

'I couldn't stick school, sir,' my informant continued, 'and I don't know why, lest it be that one man's best suited for one business, and another for another. That may be seen every day. I was sent on trial to a shoemaker, and after that to a ropemaker, for father didn't seem to like my growing up and being a bird-catcher, like he was. But I never felt well, and knew I should never be any great hand at them trades, and so when my poor father went off rather sudden, I took to the catching at once and had all his traps. Perhaps, but I can't say to a niceness, that was eleven years back. Do I like the business, do you say, sir? Well, I'm forced to like it, for I've no other to live by.' [The reader will have remarked how this man attributed the course he pursued evidently from natural inclinations, to its being the best and most healthful means of subsistence in his power.] 'Last Monday, for my dealers like birds on a Monday or Tuesday best, and then they've the week before them, – I went to catch in the fields this side of Barnet, and started before two in the morning, when it was neither light nor dark. You must get to your place before daylight to be ready for the first flight, and have time to lay your net properly. When I'd done that, I lay down and smoked. No, smoke don't scare the birds; I think they're rather drawn to notice anything new, if all's quite quiet. Well, the first pull I had about 90 birds, nearly all linnets. There was, as well as I can remember, three hedge-sparrows among them, and two larks, and one or two other birds. Yes, there's always a terrible flutter and row when you make a catch, and often regular fights in the net. I then sorted my birds, and let the hens go, for I didn't want to be bothered with them. I might let such a thing as 35 hens go out of rather more than an 80 take, for I've always found, in catching young broods, that I've drawn more cocks than hens. How do I know the difference when the birds are so young? As easy as light from dark. You must lift up the wing, quite tender, and you'll find that a cock linnet has black, or nearly black, feathers on his shoulder, where the hens are a deal lighter. Then the cock has a broader and whiter stripe in the wing than the hen has. It's quite easy to distinguish, quite. A cock goldfinch is straighter and more larger in general than a hen, and has a broader white on his wing, as the cock linnet has; he's black round the beak and the eye too, and a hen's greenish thereabouts. There's some grey-pates (young birds) would deceive any one until he opens their wings. Well, I went on, sir, until about one o'clock, or a little after, as well as I could tell from the sun, and then came away with about 100 singing birds. I sold them in the lump to three shopkeepers at 2*s*. 2*d*. and 2*s*. 6*d*. the dozen. That was a good day, sir; a very lucky day. I got about 17*s*., the best I ever did but once, when I made 19*s*. in a day.

'Yes, it's hard work is mine, because there's such a long walking home when you've done catching. O, when you're at work it's not work but almost a pleasure. I've laid for hours though without a catch. I smoke to pass the time when I'm watching; sometimes I read a bit if I've had anything to take with me to read; then at other times I thinks. If you don't get a catch for hours, it's only like an angler without a nibble. O, I don't know what I think about; about nothing, perhaps. Yes, I've had a friend or two go out catching with me just for the amusement. They must lie about and wait as I do. We have a little talk of course: well, perhaps about sporting; no, not horse-racing, I care nothing for that, but it's hardly business taking any one with you. I supply the dealers and hawk as well. Perhaps I make 12*s*. a week the year through. Some weeks I've made between 3*ls*. and 4*ls*., and in winter, when there's rain every day, perhaps I haven't cleared a penny in a fortnight. That's the worst of it. But I make more than others because I have a connection and raise good birds.'

Of Sources

OF STREET PIEMEN

London Labour and the London Poor, Volume 1, 1851, pp. 197– [Penguin ed., pp. 94–7]

London Labour and the London Poor is the work Mayhew is remembered for today. It began as a series of letters commissioned by the *Morning Chronicle* exposing the working lives and conditions of the London poor. They formed part of a wider series on the condition of the working classes across England, with correspondents reporting from the industrial towns and rural areas too. The *Morning Chronicle* was an avowedly liberal national daily newspaper, the rival of the Tory *Times*. Starting in 1849, at first the weekly letters were anonymous, credited to the 'Metropolitan Correspondent', but as their fame grew, Mayhew's authorship became known. This came as a surprise to many. He had made his name as a satirical playwright and writer, and was one of the founders of *Punch* magazine in 1841, as well as a philosopher with a treatise on education and lectures under his belt, and was also known as something of a gifted amateur scientist. In his letters he developed his trademark method of letting the people speak for themselves, building up around their accounts a detailed picture of their communities and working lives, using a range of sources, from government statistics to their own housekeeping accounts, mixed in with first-hand accounts of his visits to the places they lived. After two years he fell out with the *Morning Chronicle*, accusing them of censoring his articles because they questioned the merits of free trade for the poor, and offended some lucrative advertisers. In December 1850 he launched his own weekly series, *London Labour and the London Poor*, using his own resources, taking some of the team he had built up at the *Morning Chronicle* with him. Here he continued his work, his main focus being on the street folk, with a parallel series soon launched on prostitution. Though recognized as a unique work, and said to be selling 18,000 copies a week at its height, its finances were shaky. On 16 March 1852 the printers gained a High Court injunction against Mayhew for non-payment of fees and *London Labour* was lost in Chancery for the next four years. Only one and a half volumes on the street folk and half of the volume on prostitution had been completed. Mayhew never finished them. In 1856 his publisher, David Bogue, a long-term friend and supporter, bought the copyright and work began on a relaunch, but Bogue died that same year and the project died with him. The copyright was sold on to Griffin and Bohn in 1861. They hired their own writers to complete the work, and reissued it September 1861, to become the four-volume edition it is known as today. It was out of print by the time of Mayhew's death in 1887, and lay forgotten for decades. It was only in the 1950s that new editions were brought out and Mayhew's work rediscovered.

A BALLOON FLIGHT

The Great World of London, D. Bogue, 1856. Republished as *The Criminal Prisons of London*, Griffin and Co., 1862, pp. 8–10

This piece was first published in the *Illustrated London News* on 18 September 1852, not long after *London Labour and the London Poor* ended publication. It was republished as part of Mayhew's second series, *The Great World of London*, in 1856. Intended as an encyclopaedia of all aspects of London life and culture, an extension to his work in *London Labour* on the street folk, the series ran for under a year before collapsing through a combination of illness on Mayhew's part and the sudden death of his publisher, David Bogue. Only the introduction to the series, an overview of London, and the sections on the criminal prisons of London were ever completed. Bogue's executors tried to persuade Mayhew to continue the work, but he chose to walk away from it. Eventually, the copyright was brought by Griffin and Bohn from Bogue's executors, and the series, after some additional material commissioned by them from John Binney, was reissued in 1862 under the title of *The Criminal Prisons of London*, the name the work is known by today.

THE LONDON STREET MARKETS ON A SATURDAY NIGHT

London Labour and the London Poor, Volume 1, 1851, pp. 9–10 [Penguin ed., pp. 12–15]

Mayhew had a particular fascination for the London street markets. He saw them as the best places to observe people and how they lived their lives. They were where the poor went to do their late-night shopping. The New Cut market he describes here still exists behind Waterloo Station, albeit in reduced form. Of the other great street markets he visited, the Brill has been buried below King's Cross and Hungerford Market below Charing Cross, but Leather Lane and Whitecross markets still cling on today.

OF THE 'PENNY GAFF'

London Labour and the London Poor, Volume 1, 1851, pp. 36, 40–42 [Penguin ed., pp. 36–40]

As part of his exploration of the life of the costers, Mayhew visited their homes, pubs, theatres and dance halls (known as 'hops'). Here he visits a temporary theatre, thrown up in the streets around Smithfield. The ancient meat market was still a large open field where animals were driven through the streets of London to be sold and slaughtered. It was also the venue for a weekly donkey fair and races held by the costers. Mayhew relishes the atmosphere and the spectacle at the penny gaff. In a way he was at home here. He had started out in the 1830s in the theatre, and it was a life-long affair. He wrote *The Wandering Minstrel* in 1834, a short farce featuring a cockney love song, 'Villikins and his Dinah', and this remained a music hall favourite throughout the century. He was twenty-two, and perpetually hard up, so sold the copyright soon after for £25, losing out, as he later complained, on the £200 a year it had earned the owner since. He acted too, appearing in some of the amateur productions Charles Dickens staged. In the late 1830s he owned and managed the Queen's Theatre, off the Tottenham Court Road. In the late 1860s, he ran the theatre reviews for *The Times*. His last known venture on the stage was in the 1870s, when he co-wrote with his son, Athol, a comedy, *Mont Blanc*, which had a brief run at the Haymarket.

THE PORT OF LONDON

The Great World of London, D. Bogue, 1856. Republished as *The Criminal Prisons of London*, Griffin and Co., 1862, pp. 21–3

Mayhew stood on the balcony of Customs House to view the Port of London. To his right was London Bridge (still the medieval structure, though shorn of the houses that had adorned it), to his left the Tower of London, and across the river Southwark Cathedral and the Borough. Much of *London Labour* featured the lives of the people who earned a living here – the coal-whippers who unloaded the coal barges, the marine-store men, the dock workers, the sailors and the prostitutes – and the streets, wharves, pubs and slums either side of the Thames that were drawn to serve this hub of world trade. When the wind was in an easterly direction, the ships were unable to dock, and thousands would be thrown out of work until it changed again. The Port of London was a microcosm of the world in the centre of the metropolis, with people and goods constantly coming and going from all regions of the world. Mayhew was a part of that movement. In 1827, aged fifteen, he boarded a ship at Blackwall Export Docks and sailed as a midshipman to Calcutta.

OF TWO ORPHAN FLOWER GIRLS

London Labour and the London Poor, Volume 1, 1851, pp. 134–6 [Penguin ed., pp. 61–4]

Mayhew interviewed his subjects at the offices of *London Labour*, in his home, in the streets, in pubs or, as here, in their own homes. His visits allowed him to provide a context for their stories, and record the minutiae of their day-to-day lives. Many of his subjects were children, finding one way or another to survive in the City, and to build a family life when parents were absent. The orphaned girls and their landlady expressed the dignity and kindness of the poor, as well as their strength and individuality, qualities Mayhew encountered again and again through the testimonies he collected. They were also part of the Irish diaspora, the 'Irish Cockneys' he described as a distinctive community of the poor in

London, whose numbers were swollen after 1848 by the Irish Potato Famine.

THE TRAIN TO CLAPHAM COMMON

The Great World of London, D. Bogue, 1856. Republished as *The Criminal Prisons of London*, Griffin and Co., 1862, pp. 487–9

This view of London was new to Mayhew's generation, as the railways had cut their way through the City within living memory. They epitomized relentless progress and transition. Mayhew had been caught up in the 'Railway Mania', the speculative frenzy that accompanied the burst of railway construction in the mid-1840s. He had been part-owner of the *Iron Times*, a daily newspaper devoted to railway news, share speculation and the ethos of change they carried with them. Thousands made fortunes in the boom, only to lose it all sharply in the crash. By 1846, with his wife heavily pregnant with their second child, the *Iron Times* folded. Mayhew was left bankrupt and his villa in Parsons Green, Fulham, was raided by bailiffs. Soon after, he left with his family for the Channel Islands and sanctuary from his creditors, remaining there for three years. The rail journey to Clapham Common was taken in 1856, to visit the Surrey House of Correction, Wandsworth, as part of his coverage of the criminal prisons of London for *The Great World of London*. For that series he visited the prisons at Pentonville, Millbank (on the site of the current Tate Britain), Brixton, Clerkenwell, the Woolwich Hulks (old battleships converted to floating prisons) and Tothill Fields in Westminster. He began each account with a description of the approach to the location, and the sights, sounds and smells of the immediate world outside the walls. The journey to Wandsworth Prison was his last. The series ended abruptly, midway through the description of the prison.

OF THE STREET-SELLERS OF LIVE BIRDS

London Labour and the London Poor, Volume 2, 1851, pp. 58–66

London, the 'Great Metropolis', was the largest city in the world and in a state of constant change. The poor made their living at the physical margins of this growth, in the brickfields, the leisure gardens, the fields, as much as in the streets, sweatshops, docks and factories. Some had lifestyles that Mayhew admired for their freedom. He never romanticized them, but expressed an affinity with them, as someone who lived on the margins too. The craft and knowledge of the street-bird seller straddled the rural and the urban, the one fast consuming the other, and the fields where he lay in wait for the flocks of birds would soon be lost beneath streets and houses.

1. BOCCACCIO · *Mrs Rosie and the Priest*
2. GERARD MANLEY HOPKINS · *As kingfishers catch fire*
3. *The Saga of Gunnlaug Serpent-tongue*
4. THOMAS DE QUINCEY · *On Murder Considered as One of the Fine Arts*
5. FRIEDRICH NIETZSCHE · *Aphorisms on Love and Hate*
6. JOHN RUSKIN · *Traffic*
7. PU SONGLING · *Wailing Ghosts*
8. JONATHAN SWIFT · *A Modest Proposal*
9. *Three Tang Dynasty Poets*
10. WALT WHITMAN · *On the Beach at Night Alone*
11. KENKŌ · *A Cup of Sake Beneath the Cherry Trees*
12. BALTASAR GRACIÁN · *How to Use Your Enemies*
13. JOHN KEATS · *The Eve of St Agnes*
14. THOMAS HARDY · *Woman much missed*
15. GUY DE MAUPASSANT · *Femme Fatale*
16. MARCO POLO · *Travels in the Land of Serpents and Pearls*
17. SUETONIUS · *Caligula*
18. APOLLONIUS OF RHODES · *Jason and Medea*
19. ROBERT LOUIS STEVENSON · *Olalla*
20. KARL MARX AND FRIEDRICH ENGELS · *The Communist Manifesto*
21. PETRONIUS · *Trimalchio's Feast*
22. JOHANN PETER HEBEL · *How a Ghastly Story Was Brought to Light by a Common or Garden Butcher's Dog*
23. HANS CHRISTIAN ANDERSEN · *The Tinder Box*
24. RUDYARD KIPLING · *The Gate of the Hundred Sorrows*
25. DANTE · *Circles of Hell*
26. HENRY MAYHEW · *Of Street Piemen*
27. HAFEZ · *The nightingales are drunk*
28. GEOFFREY CHAUCER · *The Wife of Bath*
29. MICHEL DE MONTAIGNE · *How We Weep and Laugh at the Same Thing*
30. THOMAS NASHE · *The Terrors of the Night*
31. EDGAR ALLAN POE · *The Tell-Tale Heart*
32. MARY KINGSLEY · *A Hippo Banquet*
33. JANE AUSTEN · *The Beautifull Cassandra*
34. ANTON CHEKHOV · *Gooseberries*
35. SAMUEL TAYLOR COLERIDGE · *Well, they are gone, and here must I remain*
36. JOHANN WOLFGANG VON GOETHE · *Sketchy, Doubtful, Incomplete Jottings*
37. CHARLES DICKENS · *The Great Winglebury Duel*
38. HERMAN MELVILLE · *The Maldive Shark*
39. ELIZABETH GASKELL · *The Old Nurse's Story*
40. NIKOLAY LESKOV · *The Steel Flea*

41. HONORÉ DE BALZAC · *The Atheist's Mass*
42. CHARLOTTE PERKINS GILMAN · *The Yellow Wall-Paper*
43. C.P. CAVAFY · *Remember, Body . . .*
44. FYODOR DOSTOEVSKY · *The Meek One*
45. GUSTAVE FLAUBERT · *A Simple Heart*
46. NIKOLAI GOGOL · *The Nose*
47. SAMUEL PEPYS · *The Great Fire of London*
48. EDITH WHARTON · *The Reckoning*
49. HENRY JAMES · *The Figure in the Carpet*
50. WILFRED OWEN · *Anthem For Doomed Youth*
51. WOLFGANG AMADEUS MOZART · *My Dearest Father*
52. PLATO · *Socrates' Defence*
53. CHRISTINA ROSSETTI · *Goblin Market*
54. *Sindbad the Sailor*
55. SOPHOCLES · *Antigone*
56. RYŪNOSUKE AKUTAGAWA · *The Life of a Stupid Man*
57. LEO TOLSTOY · *How Much Land Does A Man Need?*
58. GIORGIO VASARI · *Leonardo da Vinci*
59. OSCAR WILDE · *Lord Arthur Savile's Crime*
60. SHEN FU · *The Old Man of the Moon*
61. AESOP · *The Dolphins, the Whales and the Gudgeon*
62. MATSUO BASHŌ · *Lips too Chilled*
63. EMILY BRONTË · *The Night is Darkening Round Me*
64. JOSEPH CONRAD · *To-morrow*
65. RICHARD HAKLUYT · *The Voyage of Sir Francis Drake Around the Whole Globe*
66. KATE CHOPIN · *A Pair of Silk Stockings*
67. CHARLES DARWIN · *It was snowing butterflies*
68. BROTHERS GRIMM · *The Robber Bridegroom*
69. CATULLUS · *I Hate and I Love*
70. HOMER · *Circe and the Cyclops*
71. D. H. LAWRENCE · *Il Duro*
72. KATHERINE MANSFIELD · *Miss Brill*
73. OVID · *The Fall of Icarus*
74. SAPPHO · *Come Close*
75. IVAN TURGENEV · *Kasyan from the Beautiful Lands*
76. VIRGIL · *O Cruel Alexis*
77. H. G. WELLS · *A Slip under the Microscope*
78. HERODOTUS · *The Madness of Cambyses*
79. *Speaking of Siva*
80. *The Dhammapada*